First published in Great Britain in 2001 by
POETRY NOW
Remus House,
Coltsfoot Drive,
Peterborough, PE2 9JX
Telephone (01733) 898101
Fax (01733) 313524

HB ISBN 0 75432 565 2
SB ISBN 0 75432 566 0

FOREWORD

Although we are a nation of poets we are accused of not reading poetry, or buying poetry books. After many years of listening to the incessant gripes of poetry publishers, I can only assume that the books they publish, in general, are books that most people do not want to read.

Poetry should not be obscure, introverted, and as cryptic as a crossword puzzle: it is the poet's duty to reach out and embrace the world.

The world owes the poet nothing and we should not be expected to dig and delve into a rambling discourse searching for some inner meaning.

The reason we write poetry (and almost all of us do) is because we want to communicate: an ideal; an idea; or a specific feeling. Poetry is as essential in communication, as a letter; a radio; a telephone, and the main criterion for selecting the poems in this anthology is very simple: they communicate.

CONTENTS

YOU WILL FORGET

I know you will forget . . .
The years will give healing . . .
Pains you know will all go
And joys be known yet . . .
And you won't remember.
When time's shades come stealing,
That love was a burning ember
When we first met!

I know you will forget . . .
The boon you are craving
From blue skies as your prize
Will quite worthless get!
You will quick regard it
As not worth the saving,
And you will quickly discard it
And soon forget!

I know you will forget
And thank me for saying
Love will pass . . . years will pass . . .
And the time Time's set
Change to livelier strain . . .
But I will be praying
That we may meet one day again . . .
I won't forget!

Dan Pugh

FROM A DAUGHTER

I often think of you
quite suddenly in brief cameos,
vivid images which focus fade,
then reappear

a smile on the edge of laughter
your gaze held in conversation
a favourite scent drifting
on a draught of air

small fragments of your wholeness
held for fleeting moments
made real by the intensity
of my longing

I often think of our goodbye
wishing it had been an embrace
instead of the hurried kiss
in flight between us

Helen Clarke

LOVE REMAINS

Look up on a winter's night
And see what you can see
A host of dusted diamonds
Upon a velvet sea
And there between the starlight
My thoughts are ever free

Listen on a summer's day
And hear what you can hear
The breezes soothing whisper
Across a crystal mere
And out along the river
My dreams are running clear

Walk along an autumn lane
And smell what you can smell
Sparkling leaves a-tumbling
In a golden swell
And in that mellow season
My spirits ever dwell

Touch the springtime showers
And feel what you can feel
The power of life emerging
Nature's driving zeal
And in that moment's pleasure
You'll know my love was real

C D Goldsmith

THE ARTIFICIAL LEG

*(A poem written in memory of Tom 'Pegleg'
my grandfather - 1892/1957)*

His leg, like the creaking of a rusty hinge
announced his coming long before he arrived;
My brother, Clive
seeking to be his 'pet',
would be first through the door so as to hug him close;
My grandfather, stubbing out his cigarette,
would kiss us both.

The leg was attached to his stockened stump
by an assortment of straps and wires;
He quickly tired
when he walked,
as movement was achieved by swinging his leg wide
in semi-circular fashion; No wonder that he talked
to everyone he met. The pause was a time to gain strength
for the next stride.

Children, cruel then, as now would laugh at his gait,
calling out 'pegleg' as he went down the road;
It was ignored
save for that time
when, with stick in hand he turned to give chase
but, losing his balance fell; He could wipe the grime
from his hands. The humiliation was more ingrained;
It was in his face.

I remember him smiling then. His was the courage
which could say, in spite of adversity, 'What the hell!'
But who can tell
what he really thought?
He would not talk about his war;
the shattered dream, the ruined life, the broken heart;
Nor did he speak, not even once
of surgeon's saw.

Of all this, and more, his leg bore witness,
encapsulating, in itself, what remained unsaid;
After he was dead
that leg still
spoke of things which, in these , my mature years,
I can better understand: It ever will
remind me of him, inspiring hope;
Sometimes tears.

Reverend Mike Shephard

REMEMBERING

I remember the way you were,
That shy sexy look, the smell of your hair.
I laugh to myself at that half-remembered joke we shared.
The way on impulse you hugged me to your chest -
And said how much you cared.

I can still feel the shape of your lips -
The memory clinging still to my fingertips.
Being so close we took turns to kiss,
All those intimacies I miss.

The thrill of seeing you as you walked my way,
Relief as you arrived - words can't say.
The memories come flooding back to me,
I smile and blush and brush away a tear.

Remembering the carefree moments
Each time together was sweet.
I remember the sunlight through the trees -
As you swept me off my feet.

In that distant time, the urgency with which we loved.
Looking back we never knew how short the time,
We had our youth and vitality,
I was only yours and you were only mine

Remember the time we couldn't bear to be apart?
The nights we spent enraptured right from the very start.
Your eyes became my windows my life reflected there -
I sank into their very depths of your hypnotic stare.

Say you remember the way things were then as well,
Say the feelings I recall were yours too when you fell.
It's just a distant past, a part of our shared lifetime.
Precious memories - I was only yours and you were only mine.

Christina Clarke

THE WORLD IS WHAT WE MAKE IT

The world is what we make it,
Look up, you're sure to find,
As wise men keep on saying,
It's all a state of mind.
Remember those two inmates
Who looked through prison bars;
One cursed the rain and watched it drain
Around mud-splattered cars,
The other gazed while his heart praised
The wonder of the stars.

The world is what we make it,
No point in thoughts of gloom,
No sense in being rigid,
Like something from the tomb.
From time to time there's someone
Who feels deprived and hurt,
His eyes don't zoom to flowers in bloom,
He only sees the dirt;
Let's be inclined to keep in mind
Peace starts within the heart.

So let your heart be giving,
Whatever drifts your way,
Relax and keep on loving,
Come what may.
The truth is sure to find us,
To seek us out and bind us,
If we but practise kindness
All the way;
Then peace will come,
Yes, peace will come to stay.

Campbell McQueen

FOLLOW MY HEART

'My dearest darling
my love for you,
I will follow my heart.
My love so true,
our love so rare
is beyond compare,
like the moon above
I will follow my heart.

As the stars, they chime
our love sublime,
I will follow my heart.
To the ends of the earth,
my life I'll give
my life to share,
our gift of love
for us to share
I will follow my heart.'

Elizabeth Anne Feeney

FLY FREE

Fly free O dream of amicable hearts,
   cast cynicism asunder -
   to relinquish joy.
Foretell O heart thy yearning desires,
Sweet harmony ascend unto your dream,
in serenity seek brotherhood
   unto the new deal.
In unison eternal all compassion comply.

Fly free O mind amid unrest abounding
   proclaim such peace amid freedoms stride,
obeisance profound hover never to lie,
in abundant lustre shine light of hope,
unto nations and beyond shout honour wide,
immortal grace to endless caress,
amid futile conflicts of angers showing
   o winds of logic show thy face.

Fly free O compassions so solace endure,
   suffocate iniquity to embellish the earth,
such paradise no dream -
   where understanding flows,
ascend to conquer valiant true hearts,
let conflict be exiled unto the deal
then upon unison for eternity to last,
shall all people bow unto peace the same.

Steve Kettlewell

YOU MAY CHOOSE

Silent is golden.
No one can deny it.
It deserves respect
From all walks of life.
Sincere, silent love is a priceless gem.
A silent prayer from de bottom of the
Heart in Heaven can be heard.

So, don't be shy, it will be fine.
You may choose.
Use either words or be mute.

But, does it matter
If you talk?
Does it matter
If your lips are silent?
Make no mistake,
Your heart is a book,
And everything that is in it
I can read - in your eyes.

Victoria E Tejedor

METAMORPHOSIS (FRIENDSHIP)

It was like a slap on the face
when you ended our relationship.
I had assumed friendship,
I had given gladly
knowing your need,
expecting nothing - but
sometimes to see your smile,
the lightness of your eye,
and to hear your voice.

But it all ended
like a squall of wind in autumn
that tears the leaves from the trees
and blows them in the dust
in eddying circles.

It is the end;
there is nothing now between us.
Within myself
I have found resources
bubbling up like a hill spring
which seeks new courses
bringing healing and refreshment,
yet containing all that has been
given and received.

Love, truth and beauty
contained in this way
and built upon
is eternal.

Beryl Johnson

THANKFUL THOUGHTS

Be thankful for the friends who love you
Be thankful for the people who support you
Be thankful for the difficulties that make you struggle
Be thankful for the strength to overcome them
Be thankful for the hardships that made you strong
Be thankful for the enemies who keep you cautious
Be thankful for the courage given by others
Be thankful for the disappointments that make you try harder
Be thankful for the life we hold
Be thankful for God up above.

Glenys M Bowell

NO MORE

No more pleasure no more pain
No more losses no more gain

No more loving no more hate
No more giving no more take

No more laughter no more tears
No more bemoan advancing years

No more sorrow no more joy
No baby girl no baby boy

No more greetings no goodbyes
No more cheating no more lies

No more ageing no more youth
No more seeking out the truth

No more good times no more bad
No more happy no more sad

No more friendships no more foes
No more joyful no more woes

No more evil no more good
No more water no more blood

No more genius no retard
No more easy no more hard

No more poets no more kings
No more playgrounds no more swings

No more vision no more face
No more no more
The Human Race.

Edward C Fairweather

GOD'S BLESSING

You came into our life only eighteen months old
With nobody to love you, hug, cuddle or hold.
You sat in your playpen, no idea what to do
The toys all around did not amuse you.
As soon as we saw you we knew from the start
That one of our family you'd soon become part.
You've now got a mummy, daddy, sister and brothers two
A grandma and grandad who all adore you.
Now you are walking and learning to talk
You play with your toys and make plenty of noise.
Off to play school with your special friend there
Samira looks after you with loving care.
You are God's blessing from above
All you needed was our devoted love.

Betty Bailey

SPECIAL SEASHELLS

When we visit the seashore we are likely to find
Some exquisite seashells, uniquely designed,
And when all the traces of seaweed and grime
Which may have built up through the passage of time
Have been rinsed away, these shells can be seen,
Their intricate beauty resplendent and clean.
Their forms may be complex and delicate too,
Imaging sea life and giving us clues
As to how each survived and the life that they led,
Whether diving or resting on the seabed.

I feel we leave shells as we pass through our lives:
Not just like bees, building honeycombs, hives.
We do leave impressions as we pass along,
Maybe our actions, our views or a song,
Or maybe an outfit which left an impression,
A heart-warming smile or a special expression.
Or maybe a scent, or a time which brought pleasure.
But each leaves a moment, a seashell to treasure.
Let's do our utmost to leave shells which feel warm,
Which do not hold malice, or anger, or scorn
But carry an aura of fairness and love
And show our true selves like a well-tailored glove.

Emma Louise Taylor

JOURNEY

Giant iron girders passing by,
Cold steel structure, stronger than I,
Takes me away, far from you,
The Lomond Hills fade from view.

A battered suitcase, tied with string,
I'm a little used like that old thing,
In a train going down the line,
Turn and look, for one last time.

Leave the rooftops of the city,
As a stranger view each green field,
The steel rails sing a song of pity
To soothe a wound that's never healed.
They sing a song of life's adventure,
For the traveller, perhaps, a happier day,
Though the spirit is bruised
And the heart is broken,
You will journey forever,
That's what they say.

Iron girders passing by,
Cold steel bridge, stronger than I.
In a train going down the line, Lucy
Turn and look, for one last time.

Scott Martin

JUST FOR A TIME

Bravely we must
face our fate
The crisis of life
to bear -
'moving on' - to
overcome
The loneliness of fear.

To forget oneself
and look around,
So plainly there to see -
'Always another being
in a plight much worse
than me.'

Then each new day - as
we venture forth
God gives us harmony -
For we place our trust
and His guiding hand
unravels life's mystery

'That death comes to all -
that we might live
in purest spiritual grace -
So just for a time - you
must 'move on' -
Let your loved-one Rest in Peace.

Mary Skelton

ALL MY LOVE

I love you all
And know you all love me.
Even though we argue
And often disagree.

When times are rough
And we haven't enough.
We'll grumble and we'll groan.

But in our hearts
We'll look and see,
Our love has fairly grown.

So think about each other daily
And life will always stay
A happy place without a worry
With love in abundance each day.

Wendy Scott

LOVE IS - LOVE CAN

Love is a passion,
That comes from within,
Triggered by emotions,
Or a little whim!

Love is all things,
To each and everyone,
Jealousy and heartache,
All rolled into one.

Love can be fulfilling,
Love can be despair,
Love can be everything,
If the one you love is there.

So take the love that's within you,
And find the one that cares,
For love is more fulfilling,
If that love is shared!

Howard Croston

BEYOND THE SILENCE

Watching quietly the distant city's lights shine so bright,
Nothing can disturb my sweet silence of night.
Miles away from the city, you can't hear a sound,
Still the nightlife's already started, street crowds gather round.
Starting parties of wild dancing, that will last all night long.
The strangest people blend together and they seem to belong.
With no care in the world, they start to merge into one.
Leaving all reality so their mind starts to run.
All their minds are gone and lost in their creation of madness,
It's now controlling all their minds can they come back through
the hardness.
It's a fight within themselves, you can't get your will power elsewhere,
For I found mine within my heart, so I'm in the distance and not there.

Kirsteen Driver

A LIFE WELL LIVED

Shed not the tears of bitterness
Cast not the nets of grief,
Stay not in mental wilderness.
For life is short and brief

But roam in verdant dale and glen,
In flowery vales of thought,
Be healing balm unto all men
A garland finely wrought.

Be a bright light to their distress,
The beacon ray of hope,
The gentle word to steer and bless,
In their dark pit, a rope.

And thus the day your eyes will close
Will be a day of rest,
The joy that a good conscience knows
Is password to the blessed.

And then with spirit eyes you'll see
The happiness you created,
The gracious soul will then be free:
Pure light regenerated.

Emmanuel Petrakis

SOMEONE SPECIAL

The dreary rain clouds fill the sky, no glint of sunshine to be seen,
A weary figure, passing by, recalls the dreams that might have been,
The memories of long ago, a calendar of four-score years,
Of things which others cannot know, of blood and sweat, and
                                                    toil and tears.

His weary shoulders, bent with age, are hunched against the
                                                    driving rain,
No longer does he earn a wage, his pension now his only gain.
His needs are few, his future bleak, 'The Reaper' not too far behind,
Till in a shop he'll shelter seek, where smiles are warm, and
                                                    words are kind.

And as that cheery voice he hears, 'Hello, and how are you today?'
He'll seem to shrug away the years, old eyes with mischief start to play,
For here, away from outside's chill, his body warming to her smile,
She makes him feel a human still, and so he'll linger for a while.

And when at last he moves away, to face the world outside again,
It seems to be a better day, despite the cold and driving rain,
And sometimes too, this winsome Miss, 'ere he continues on his way,
Will let him steal a gentle kiss, to warm his heart, and make his day.

The sands of time must ever run, and life indeed for all must cease.
But when man's life on earth is done, and preachers bid him,
                                                    'Rest in peace.'
The deeds he did, the things he saw, forever on the winds are blown,
That 'special gift' for evermore, one final love, enjoyed, and known . . .

D K Brough

LOVE AND UNDERSTANDING

My little grandchild is not very well.
Off her sore throat and sore ears she can't tell.
As little Beth is just eighteen months old
Mum loves and understands her as she has her to hold.

She is covered with a rash so red,
The doctor says keep her in bed.
He says it's a virus she has got
Mum has to cool down as she gets very hot.

It's a very worrying time as we love her a lot
She doesn't understand as she is such a tiny tot.
We can only pray to God above
And have love and understanding for the little one we love.

E Greig

THE WAY

My spirit is soaring
As free as a bird,
I see so much beauty
In God's wondrous world.
I feel Him watch o'er me,
I reach to the sky,
Peace, hope within me,
His love never dies.

I watch the birds flying,
As they wing their way
To safe roosting places,
At the end of the day.
No less has He promised
To those who have faith,
That peace will go with them
To the ends of the earth.

So we should never worry,
For right all will be,
As our paths are mapped out,
As we'll surely see.
If we follow our Guide,
And pay heed to His call,
Our steps may still falter,
But He won't let us fall.

Barbara Henry

THE EBBING TIDE

The news dates the playground
And the radio deafens love songs.

Entertainment drifts
Like the broken pastime of growth,

Honey-flavoured stories
Crinkle memories

Like flowers grown
In foreign newspapers.

Winter is no different
In its shelter of snow.

A sea of capsules ebbs
On medicated pebbles.

Marylène Walker

ANGELS' WINGS

Oh, how frail the human heart
How easily it's torn apart
It only takes one thoughtless word
Directed straight, or overheard.
For love is such a fragile thing,
Like fairy dust or angels' wings.
Don't let your love get swept away
You'll find yourself alone one day
And that's when it will hit you most
When love will haunt you as a ghost.
I've loved and lost, and loved again
And had a heart that's filled with pain.
But now I have a heart that's light
It feels just like a bird in flight.
I have you Love, to thank for this
So let me seal it with a kiss.

Stewart Potter

DISCLOSURE

Behind the curtain of our hearts
The truth requires that all be known
And peace rewards courageous trust
When to another all is shown.

Love alone makes trusting safe
The gifts and skill to listen and care;
Time alone empowers that love
Creating every chance to share.

The residue of sin remains
But it is known for what it is:
The purging of confession's flow:
Moments of pain; a life of bliss.

John Rae Walker

A SECRET DEAR

A secret dear I've ever kept,
In silence do I grieve,
Lest your heart should e'er forget
That precious moment when we met.

Destined maybe to never meet you
After all these years;
How lonely, Girl, my heart is blue,
How strong my love - how strong, how true.

Peter Jeevar

I'LL ALWAYS BE THERE FOR YOU

My friend is hurt, is sad.
Should I stay with old chichè
'Time will make it better'
Or keep away all together?

The best thing for me to do
Is to be near you when you're sad
Let you hear the words I say,
'I'll always be there for you'
Always there till the weeping stills
And light returns to your eyes,
Always there till the pain slips away
And springtime returns to your heart.

Sister M Renshaw

TREASURES OF A RAINBOW

Treasures of a rainbow
found deep within your heart.
Promises of life to share
Such love then to impart.

Much hope for the future
Great faith with you alway
Courage for tomorrow
Mem'ries ever to stay.

Happiness does flourish
Stars twinkle down so fair
Colourful days bring delight
All glories everywhere.

Peace to find forever
And such love which has no end.
The eternal light sparkles
On this you may depend.

Margaret Jackson

THREE LITTLE WORDS

There are three little words
So often hard to say
If only we had the courage
It would be mere child's play.

Yes its hard to show our feeling
It seems so absurd
Yet it is so simple
With three little words.

They can mend many a friendship
And many a small tiff to
So what are those little words
Just say I love you.

D A Sheasby

OUR OTHER FAMILY

We have another family,
The family at our church,
And when we need a helping hand
We have not far to search;
There's shopping trips and feeding cats
And car lifts to the vet,
To church and other distant parts
And friendly smiles and chats:
We all can offer some small thing
To help each other out,
And this is what our 'family'
Is really all about.

Daphne Foreman

DISCOVERY

In turning away
I came to stay.
In trying to escape
I was bound.
In standing alone
I found friendship.
In trying to hide
I was found.

Through hate
I found love.
Through anger
I found peace.
Through bondage
I found freedom.
And through capture
I found release.

In chaos
I found a calm.
In denial
I found what was true.
In letting go
I found contentment.
Through prayer
I found you.

J Kirkpatrick

MOTHER'S DAY

Flowers and chocolates, wine and love,
I show her more of the above.

I love my mother she has the loving touch,
she is caring and loving and does so much.

She cheers me up, when I am down,
she tells me to smile when I wear a frown.

She's always there when I make mistakes,
she'll never change me no matter what she takes.

She knows I love her with all my heart,
and forever in this life we'll never part.

Bobbie Wood

WHAT IS THIS THING?

You can get it
From someone else.
This you nurture,
It's very valuable.
It's a sure thing,
Just there.
You can share it
When needed or wanted.
You don't chose that someone.
It just happens.
Having it can be nice
Or immovably painful.
Right people can be bad,
It makes no difference.
They still get it
On demand.
It's always there,
On tap, for free
But it can't be bought
For gold.
You can't take it with you,
Leave it behind,
Put it on hold,
It makes no difference.
Abuse seldom harms it,
Nor does it wear out.
It needs no servicing
And endures for ever.

Pauline Boncey

PEACE

There's a castle on a mountain surrounded by the greenest trees
Wondrous flowers like you would not believe.
There's happiness in there peace and love
A castle so big high above.
There's a castle on a mountain with a path made of gold
It's a long and bumpy road, you've a heavy load.
There's a castle on a mountain with the most wondrous gates
Trying to get there for so long and hope I'm not too late.
There's a castle on a mountain no guards to protect
They're not needed I'll get there if I'm let.
I've been walking so long trying to be strong.
There's a castle on a mountain, joyous and true
No lies or deceit no criticising all that you do.
I can see the gate
I can feel I'm close it's never too late.
I'll be there soon I've earned that right
I've tried so hard, put up a fight.
There's a castle on a mountain strong and steadfast
I'll get through the gates bad memories and pain will be in my past.
There's a castle on a mountain where I can rest my weary life
Unburden my cares and forget the days of strife.
Where I can smile once again and hold you close
I'll not miss you then, you'll not be a ghost.
There's a castle on a mountain where love is not compared,
No wars and fighting, everything is shared.
Where I can be me
Pure love you can feel and see.

Yeti

IN THE DREAMTIME

As I trudged the path beneath the trees
In my despair I kicked the leaves.
Even though these woody boughs have shed their leaf
As if in tears to share my grief -
To spare my eyes from all those tears, so that I may see
My sweet darling other part of me.
For here in this winter of stormy skies
Beneath these fading flowers, forever more, her body lies.
For in the dreamtime is now where she sleeps,
Where within my mind these thoughts do creep.
If only she could have stayed
To live with me beyond this grave,
So that once again, I could see her smile,
To live with me just once more awhile.
But if only wishes could come true,
If only I could be with you,
For all I have are my silent tears,
To close my eyes and count the years,
Until one day I may hope to find,
That the Lord had now changed His mind;
To bring His peace and let me stay
In that place so far away.
There to see my darling love
In that final Heaven above . . .
    In the dreamtime.

Eric Day

LOVE

We claim the working Grace of God
    that the Apostles had
the proclamation of our Christ
    deep joy which makes us glad.

Robert D Shooter

LOVE IS

Love is caring at first sight,
Love is wanting in the night.
Love is gently touching hands,
Love is asking no demands.
Love is just a gentle smile,
Love is needing all the while.
Love is knowing that you care,
Love is wishing you were there.
Love is gladness in my heart,
Love is pain when we're apart.
Love is gentle, love is true,
Love is what I feel for you.

Marie Elliott

RELATIVE RELATIONSHIP

Trapped in a cell though you keep the key
be kind to yourself and set your mind free.
You cried you heart out
confused full of doubt.
Life kicked you so often
your teeth fell out,
Your confidence crumbled
for so often bruised
Vulnerable when giving
for so easily used
You met me one Sunday
you stayed in your shell
It was apparent that you had been through hell
I offer you comfort in words I tell
I flip my coin in a wishing well
For where you have been
I visited as well
I pulled myself from drowning
Now my life is swell
You can achieve if you just believe
Keep on going you will succeed.

John Beals

HOWEVER SIMPLE

I find that when my heart does weep,
And anger wells within my soul.
The way to soothe my hurt is clear . . .
In country lanes to take a stroll.
No sound except the call of birds
From arching trees a-drip with rain.
Mist hovering above the stream
Reminds that Autumn's here again.
Still in the hedgerows, shining white
The nettle droops its pristine bells.
The yarrow blushing, softly pink
Creation's story simply tells.
Sudden clamour from noisy beaks,
A rushing sound of beating wings,
When overhead a wedge of geese
Honking southward, swift yearning brings.
Could I but leave in soaring flight
And put behind all fretful deeds,
Fly ever onward through the skies
To where my whimsy's fancy leads!
The simple sounding things are hard,
For I in sorrow, earthbound stay,
To try to cope with doubt and fear
And drop my tears along the way.

E Balmain

THAT GOLDEN GLOW - PART THREE

When morning came he ran outside
to greet the blood red sun,
the dew winks with a manic glee.

To breakfast, to feast upon a crust,
a piece of discarded rindless cheese,
drinking on the spindrift of early morning breeze.

Gathering morsels of ripest nuts and berries,
cheeks fat and bloated to the maximum,
he comes before her hole and lays his treasures down.

Calling softly he invites her to come and eat,
she has anticipated his call
and emerges bright and sparkling.

After the greetings of mutual affection,
the love lick of ears, whiskers and snout,
she eats of the feast presented with adulation.

And now on for dessert, away on to the cornfield
where the golden glow shone to the infinite,
up the stalks to banquet on the lush, ripe seeds.

Replete our lovers curl to a single ball,
corn heads gently wave overhead,
in the lush undergrowth, bodies intertwined, they sleep.

Within this land where dream and reality weave,
one dreams of marriage, the other freedom,
but both dream of the love they prize.

Jump, leap, cuff, nudge and butt,
our pair play amongst the stalks,
a game of tag leaves them breathless.

No stoat nor weasel in Elysium,
hawk nor kestrel casting evil shadow,
only the glow is known, only the glow exists.

Robin Colville

KINGDOM OF HEAVEN

A life shared, with each other
Now left only, with memories of the heart,
Two - who were as one,
By life's chosen destiny, now apart.

Till meeting - once again,
In a place, which time has never owned,
A kingdom - known as heaven.
Where the one who gave,
- Now receives in return
The ones he knows, to be his own.

Bakewell Burt

Understanding You . . .

If you take my hand I can make it alright,
If you have a worry don't sit up alone all night,
Talking is a help method, to communicate is the key,
I'm here to help by just being me,
It's alright to let me into your heart,
Didn't I always say that right from the start?

If you open your mind let all your worries go,
Instead of inside your head letting them grow,
Don't push away the feeling of love it's too strong,
To you I everlastingly belong,
It's not very easy if you don't know how,
But now is the time I will make it right somehow.

I know sometimes the world can be a nasty place,
Funny old gender this human race,
Some can attack with their words brutally mean,
And through this experience I have been,
Some can use the power of the mind,
To mentally destroy some of mankind.

I know that you put the stars in the sky for me,
Trust in me and us and together we can be,
All that you ever wanted, needed or desired before,
Don't go shutting this heavy old door,
I'm offering you my love it's pure and so right,
So that you can let me hold you all through the night.

Camilla Yardy

V DAY

Peace comes when the heart is true
Love and cherish make not blue
Understanding, all is in lieu.

Geof Farrar

NEVER GIVE IN

Do not put yourself
Into endless despair
I can assure you my *friend*
There's (always) someone to care.

Whether it be your age
Disability or your creed
Help is always at hand
For your never-ending need.

I know this to be clear
Also that it is true
It comes from (my) experience
That I share this comfort with you.

For take a look around you
Listen to radio, watch TV
There are lots of poor and sorry souls
Who do suffer, more than you or me.

Do not fold yourself away
Like an Christmas card into a drawer
Hold your head above the water
See hope and happiness, come to you once more.

Have faith in your ability
Take hope into your stride
Whatever your circumstances may be
Look forward, with love and pride.

Rob Passmore

UNTITLED

One prayer, One song,
One long, long road of many travels.

I met a man
whose cloak he offered
to keep me shielded
from the winds.

He spoke little to me,
yet told me a great deal;
We spoke mostly in the higher realm.

He carried a long pole
to remind him of his inner uprightness
as his back was doubled and bent.

His stance was solemn, silent, and of solace.
I felt afeared, 'case he did not take kindly
to my accompanying him.

But a little light
rose in his eyes
as he read my fear,
and I stayed with him.

We walked many miles as one,
he never tired
and spoke rarely of the pain I know he had.

At length we crossed a little stream
and it took us to New Ground.
He hesitated, but soon confirmed the pace.

New lights shone
and I asked him how he Knew.
One prayer he said,
One song,
and one long long road of many travels.

Lucy Trevitt

HAVE FAITH

If you feel the sky is always grey
Those dark clouds will one day blow away,
Then you will see the sky is painted blue
Painted especially just for you.

If you feel afraid through the darkest night
Just think of that big star, shining so bright,
I know it will guide you and show you the way
Till the morning sun brightens up your day.

If you feel alone to fight your fight
Ask your God to keep you right,
Then reach out for that helping hand
Then you will know *we* understand . . .

Brian Ducker

MY DEAR LOVE MOTHER

A lifetime of love and beyond
the threshold, hovering over us
As does the kestrel who swoops
Suddenly and catches his prey.

I am caught in your unseen heart
Feeling the echoes of your love
Reaching out from across the Millennia
To capture my soul and pin it down.

It is loathe to be pinned and flutters free,
As bright as a peacock, painted lady or fritillary
Alighting as it will on bush, bud or briar
Proclaiming love for all to see.

You are free of this wearisome world,
But still watch over me and mine,
Bringing comfort, well-being and love
To those who struggle in nature's claw.

The kestrel is indeed your bird,
That swoops and hovers over us;
Overshadowing and eagle-eyed
Missing nothing and knowing all.

Gabrielle Hopkins

WE'RE SO DIFFERENT, BUT SHE'S MY FRIEND

I have a friend, who I can see
Has had a much harder life than me.
We were going away for a little while
To my brother's in Bristol, quite a few mile.
But Betty had a cataract removed from her eye
Barely in time and she wondered why?
She has lost nearly all her neighbours,
Her brother as well, but she does more labours
In her church, than me, a regular plan
She does her job, whenever she can.
Last year at Christmas it was the same,
But as soon as possible out she came.
Now I have an alarm system that speaks
I've been quite happy for weeks and weeks.
I don't force her to come out, I think she knows,
If I'm out late she worries, I suppose
And sometimes she says quite laughingly
That she is looking after me.
She loves her nights out of course, I know
That she would be rather worried to go
If she didn't have transport to take her there,
And I hope at last she knows that I care.
Yes, and also I hope that she can see
That I know that she thinks a lot about me.
So I wish that our arguments will cease
Leaving love and understanding and peace.

Doreen Parsons

LOVE SONG

Every waking moment brings back memory of you
That bliss when we meet and fantasy comes true
When chance allows and I stare into the bedroom of your eyes
The sweet caress I feel like giving you never dies.

When you whisper in my ear that this must be wrong
Truth has to shout out that my feelings are strong
The stolen touch of your velvet hand gives me ecstasy
And I can't believe the power of the man that you bring out in me.

I don't remember having felt this way before
Just to have you near me makes me want you more
Never dreamed a dream that on waking I would feel
So touched, so moved, so real.

Do you know the feelings you bring out in me
Were only meant for angels not for a man like me
And when you sigh and say you can't believe that this is true
Can't you sense the addiction between me and you.

You make me smile when I think of that champagne cork
And I laugh at the way on the telephone we talk
Of bluebells and body smells from our warm embrace
As the canopy of leaves spills light all across your face.

Memory sucks in all the feelings of emotion
As I ride the tide that I feel inside like an ocean
All my yearning has the strength of a wave in a storm-wrecked sea
Like my love for you so naturally.

Frank Samet

INSPIRATION

There are many unique things, that make up a person's life,
But there is one thing in particular, that we cannot deny
That is love, the love of our family
Or the love of our friends.
If we receive this, as well as can give it
It can give us inspiration to do so many things
And when I sat down and thought about it
I thought of how much I have been inspired
How much some people truly mean to me
So I got my pen and wrote about it.

We would all love the money, the adoration or the fame
But without the love of our closest ones
All these things would not keep us sane.
We need to feel appreciated
Like we mean something to someone
Someone who can give us the will to succeed
Like that I have received from my Dad and my Mum!

Rachael Turnage

THE UNIVERSE AND EARL GREY

This city. This street. This house. This room.
Five to three on the twelfth of June.
I stand at the window, drinking tea.
Time, like an ever-rolling sea,
Trundles before me and behind,
As insubstantial as the wind.

\#

Behind me, enormous, over my shoulder,
A desolate, spinning, barren boulder.
No speck of green on the ashy plain
Before millions of years of wind and rain.
I stand at the window and sip Earl Grey,
And look out beyond the Milky Way,
Beyond Neptune's suns and Pluto's moons
Spinning their weird, ethereal tunes.

Surely it must be evidence
Of God's divine omnipotence,
Ineffable wisdom and infinite grace,
At this particular point in space
And this particular moment in time,
Mirabile dictu, that I am?

Norman Bissett

A Broken Heart

When fate decrees, that it's time to part,
And all that's left, is a broken heart.
With those promises that were made
And the plans, so finely laid.

Now all in tatters, you don't know why
Tears flowing, as you softly cry,
Asking where, oh where did I go wrong?
What did I do? your only song.

Hope gone and all alone,
Standing alone in the broken home.
Which way to turn, you do not know,
As down a lonely road you go.

Don't despair, 'cos you're not alone,
Others before you, have had to roam
And search their hearts to find the way
To live and start another day.

It will be hard, I do not lie,
So lift your eyes up to the sky.
Give a little prayer for hope,
Let help come from other folk.

They will show the way to go
Then peace and pleasure again you'll know.

George W Bailey

FREEZE-FRAME FLAME

Reaching, perusing, for a deep
Dark night to reap.
Debauchery,
And more, I see.
Tawny, tantalising, so bright,
So warm and right.
Pretty, spangly,
Shifty, risky;
However, subtle, calm and sure
Inside I'm cured.
Darkening fire,
Vanquish, expire.

Alison Standish

LOVING OPTIMISM

I fold my arms around you
like a cloak to keep you warm,
if on winter nights you're sad
wrap it close tight,
use it to protect you
when life's chill winds
blow round you,
when fog and frost attack you
as you walk into the night.

We all need extra caring
when our dreams are looking jaded,
when it seems that nothing in our lives
will ever turn out right,
surely somewhere out there
is a never-ending rainbow,
although it's hard to find it -
we must not give up the fight.

Doreen Dean

DREAMS

As we lay down to rest
At the eve of our day
Free at last of our earth suits
To the heavens we soar
Through dreamland
And beyond
On a voyage we go
Flying high on clouds
Through to the stars
Way up high
Eyelids tight shut
Eyes open wide
To times of our lives
To revisit once more
Happiness reigns free from my chains
Times gone by lived again in the sky
No barriers there
No laws of our land
Together once more we walk hand in hand
The love we once shared
So vivid, so real
I hold out my hand
To touch it, to feel
Too soon daylight beckons
To my earth suit I must now return
And in my shackles and chains
I live through my days
Till once more
The light will mellow and dim
And to dreamland I'll go
Absolved of my sin.

Helen Walker

A Plea For Peace

All we ask
is a chance to live
a fruitful life in peace,
a little thought
and understanding,
and wars would surely cease.

We need to
fight a little less,
and talk a little more;
Try to see
their point of view,
and there need be no war.

Does that seem
like Utopia? A dream
that can't come true?
Or a goal
that's really possible,
it's up to me and you!

So let us try
to use what talents
we may each possess,
so our children
can expect a future,
and the world know happiness.

James Kimber

FIFTY FIVE YEARS WITH NO WORLD WAR

Since I retired I reminisce quite a lot
I think about the good and bad memories I've got
Every year on the eleventh of November
Death and destruction, I will remember.
The war in Italy I was in from the start
The invasion of Sicily, which I was a part
Bombardment and attack from air, the constant fears
The whole campaign was to take almost two years.
As an RE I was building bridges, or clearing mines
I forget how many were built in those times
The enemy blew up bridges, then set their gun sights
So they could shoot at us, when we built bridges at nights.
Sometimes we advanced, twenty miles in one go
Other times our advances were very, very slow
Not once did we ever have to retreat
Our enemies we were determined to beat
Eventually we reached Austria in May forty-five
As uninjured survivors, were very much alive.
The war over we were sent back to Trieste
And we soon found out it wasn't for a rest
We had to protect the port from the Yugoslavs
The port and area, they thought they should have
With the best of our ability, we kept them at bay
And they are still causing trouble, to this day.
Armistice Day I watch the telly and shed a tear
Was there really any need for this anger and fear

Now when I visit Germany, some aged men I see
I wonder if they were the ones, who were shooting at me.

George E Woollard

ETERNAL PEACE AT LAST

My memory of war was my aunty's scream
As the bombs fell now seems like a dream
My grandfather's only photograph burnt in chip shop fire
My aunty and uncle called away on hire
At the start a tyrant responsible for it all
When it started they stood ten feet tall.
Once again the large movement of refugees
Never ceasing, not at ease.
That war and desperation brought to their knees
To church and to prayer those who fought on both sides did they care
Or were they totally unaware
It started with two on a boundary dispute
Over hundreds of years brought many a recruit
Language, dialect sounding voice, now separate
Where before they were mates.
Happy people now later
We have seen it all again
The result the same
When are we going to learn love?
The symbol of peace is the dove
The end of war not on lease
Then we shall have eternal peace.

Allan John Mapstone

ONE LOVE, ONE HEART

When I was in my early years
I went through life without a care
So here I stand at the altar now
Frozen to the spot and wondering how
To say 'I do' when I want to say 'No'
My legs are jelly, my brain is dough.
I know what I am doing is so wrong
The guests are here, it's been planned for so long
To run away I wouldn't dare
To face the truth that is out there.
A good little wife is not for me
I cry inside 'I want to be free.'
Lift up my veil and turn to him
I shake inside from limb to limb
The words come out but there's no heart
There is no love so soon to part
Her one true love is looking on
Not knowing his heart and hers are one.
The day is over and she is there
New husband laid beside her without a care
Knowing the marriage would never last
She sits and looks back on her past
But now together no more to part
They share one love and one heart.

Linda Cotton

TO PUPPY

Your life, so young
I almost envy you.
Your big, wide eyes and
Inquisitive nature
Make you such a
Special and unique treasure.

Your afternoon naps
And warm
Friendly face
Make me
Love you lots,
As I embrace
Your little tiny
Furry body
Protecting you,
Constantly.

Kim Stretton

HOUR OF DARKNESS

Here I lay in my bed
Still I hear what's being said
As the hour of darkness is closing
I no longer find myself opposing
All around the sound of tears
If only they knew I have no fears
All I feel is calm and peace
My life on earth soon to cease
Out of the darkness into the light
Now I have my destiny in sight
Choirs of angels all above
My heart filled with warmth and love
Voices, fading, the light growing dim
Realising now, I'll soon be with Him
I leave behind the grief and sorrow
With our Lord, I'll be tomorrow.

Gillian Levesley

PEACE IS A TREE

P   is for the Poplar tree
E   is for the Eucalyptus leaf
A   is for the Alder tall
C   is for sweet Cedar and Conifer
E   is for the Elderflower berry
    All these trees can be found in forest glade,
    Where a broken promise once was made,
    To find a true love notwithstanding,
    Fills me with love, peace and understanding.

Alan Pow

THINGS

What do I think of things?
Precious, valuable, glorious things.
Things forgotten, things ill-gotten
Things that clutter, things that glisten,
Things that ensure you do not listen,
To your heart and the Spirit within.

Things that make you feel secure,
Things you think they will endure,
Things you soon forget,
Things that hold you yet,
And will not let you forget.
Youth spent wandering in mind, soul and body.

Things that take you back to youth,
Things that seem so often cute,
Yet on reflection so absolute,
Things you simply can't do without,
Yet on the inside your still voice shouts.

In later years you learn that things internal are what matter,
No matter how much others flatter the outside
Just take a moment to listen to the youth natter
About the things that once mattered to you and smile . . .

Dalia Alexander

HAVE A HEART

With all the hatred, jealousy and greed
Surrounding us every day
Caring for others should be paramount to us
Should they go astray.

People set out to do their best
But their progress is governed by fate
Grasp the situation with both hands
Before it is too late.

So if one stumbles and makes a mistake
Help them to succeed and live
Don't disregard them and cast them aside
For they all have a lot to give.

Philip O'Leary

GREEN HILLS

Over the sea in Ireland
Where many a heart suffers pain
Over the hills in Ireland
Where it always seems to rain.

But clean and fresh are the green hills
That be calling you home again
For fresh, new minds in your land
Will help rebuild its fame.

Reach out with love, not war
Let's talk of peace for evermore
So you worship a different God
That's fine by me, it's not odd.

Your God and mine both want the same
To share with love and peace their aim
Let's bring back the matrimony
Begin again the harmony.

So let's grow up young lads
And put fresh new life in Ireland
To roam with peace again
It's fresh, green hills of fame.

J Friday

POST ARMAGEDDON PARADISE

After Armageddon, God's holy *war*
All Earth shall be as it was before
Satan tempted the first humans to eat the apple
Off the Tree of Knowledge of good and evil.

All nations no more, all humans immortal
The dead resurrected and all living normal
Lions and tigers eating grass like cows
All people speaking one language, unlike now.

Technology, doing nothing but good
No room for James Bond or even Robin Hood
No illness or crime, no doctors or cops
Satan in the abyss ready for the chop.

For one thousand years Jesus Christ will rule
Then Satan will be freed to tempt the fool
But then the Lord will destroy Satan forever
And we will all live happily ever after.

Study the Holy Bible fast
From Genesis to Revelation
For all its prophesies will come to pass
Soon the Lord will be rid of Satan.

H G Griffiths

ENVIRONMENT R I P

Over the years, our world must change
As we ravage and damage
Each vale and range;
Don't go seeking your childhood's haunt -
It's shrivelled and dwindled,
Grown sterile and gaunt.

Over the years, we've watched you die,
As we scramble and gamble,
Crass greed in our eye;
No use looking for wildlife now -
It's poisoned and blighted
By crimes we allow.

Nature cried, 'Mercy!' - we all closed our ears,
Ignoring imploring,
Intent on careers,
While our rivers ran foul,
And our great oceans died;
No hope of redemption
For life crucified.

Look at these pictures - see here, what's extinct,
Largesse for the needy
Pushed over the brink
By blind desecration, insatiable vice,
No thought for tomorrow . . .
A vain sacrifice.

Beryl M Smith

THE GAVEL FALLS

An Oxford man - true
Shrewd with words - logic thinking
rules were never broken or bent
a crossword lies unfinished
finally in college cloister
evil triumphed over good
no more opera - books - fine wine
the last pint of real ale is pulled.
A connoisseur is no more
the dreaming spires that once inspired
mysteries - still lie unsolved
it's a rainy night - the question's why?
No answers to hand - only car keys
to those who knew him
he was a good copper matey
the end of the final chapter.

David Charles

THOU, ALLAH, IN MELODIOUS TIME

We do await Thee, (Thine kingdom art the freedom-come)
Whilst time be passing paradise nears.
Time, keepeth faith and destiny.
The Lord, in time, in harmony, passing, passing, passing.
Paradise nearing, nearing, coming.
We may await Thee ever after time, passed, passed,
await Thine majesty in hope.

Parivash Jeelani (12)

IN MEMORY OF KEITH

He was a man
Who was a friend
He was kind
He was considerate
To the end.

A love for animals
He always had
When Sam his spaniel
Was so ill
Keith could not believe it until
The vet said
'It's best to put Sam to sleep'
Keith's health was
So hard to keep
How the pain
Used to make him weep.

But time passed
Keith wanted another dog
To have a home
So it would never feel alone
A golden retriever
Came to stay
For twelve years
They grew together
Going out in all sorts of weather.

Twelve years passed by
Mack the dog became ill
To the vets
He was took
How Keith
Needed some luck.

Mack was put down
On that day
He had cancer
In a very bad way
Keith's health suffered yet again
He tried so hard
To ease the pain
That he got another dog again.

A mongrel called Kim
Who had been roaming the streets
Hoping a kind person
She would meet
Keith came along
That wonderful day
Keith used to enjoy
Watching Kim play.

But he too
Got so ill
I can hear his laughter still
He passed over
On a December day
Kim would not be walking
Streets again, no way.

She's with me now
With other dogs I have
But sometimes
She looks really sad
I think she knows
Keith will be watching her
From heaven above
Still be giving her
Plenty of love.

Trisha Moreton

MY BELLE

It's been seven years of hell
Since I lost my dear Belle
The light of my life
Snuffed out like a candle
I miss her every minute
Of every hour in the day
Sometimes I wished that I could die
I was always a fighter
But this is a battle I cannot win
It's true what they say
Laugh and the world laughs with you
Cry and you cry alone
So you carry on laughing on the outside
And crying on the inside.
When I am not wallowing in my misery
I can count my blessings
The fact that she was the only woman
In this world that I ever wanted
And that I was lucky enough
To get her for my wife.
She was my rock, my tower of strength
When she died I was bereft
My reason for living had gone
Without the support of my family and friends
I might have been tempted to end it all
But it seems that fate will not let me
I have undergone a triple bypass
Which gives me a second chance at life
How I wish that she was here
To share my new-found health
But as they say someone who lives on in your heart
Never dies, but remains, my sweetest Belle.

James Rodger

TO GEOFF

I think about you, every day
And miss you - more than words can say.
I didn't always understand -
That this was life, how it was planned.

So many times I'd like to say,
I'm sorry that it went that way,
But underneath it all, I know
We both could feel that inner glow!

You used to say I didn't care,
But sometimes it was hard to bear.
We had our ups and downs, it's true
But then, I could depend on you.

The garden looks so dull and bare
It's missing all your tender care.
The house is lonely - so am I,
The car has gone - I have to cry.

But never mind, that's life they say
It goes on in the same old way.
The years we had just flew along,
I still remember - 'Our Song'.

I'll get by and so will you,
I'm glad that you are happy too.
And thank you for the signs you give,
So nice to know that you still live!

I know we meet in dreams at night
The way you used to hug me tight!
One day perhaps, we'll find the key -
To the way it was, for you - and me!

Joan Radmall

RAYMOND (1959)

We miss you in the autumn, 'twas in November you were born,
you brought such love and joy to me and now we are all forlorn.

We miss you in the winter, when snowflakes gently fall,
at Christmas with the family, we miss you most of all.

When spring comes round, we are very sad, for then you went away,
and left us all to mourn for you, we miss you every day.

You always were so kind to us, we had so many happy years,
we never thought that suddenly, it would all end in tears.

You did not know, how much we cared, we never really said
but yet, if only we had realised, we should now have no regret.

Every day we think of you and wish that you were here,
to enjoy the lovely springtime and your family so dear.

Dora M Beswick

MY BROTHER

Not too tall with blue, blue eyes
A smile like the sun up in the skies
He's kind and gentle, fair of face
Happy and sad, like the human race
     He's my brother.

Dark shadows daunted his peaceful life
It was all uphill with trouble and strife
Smiles turned to frowns, truths turned to lies
Too much to do, before one dies.
     He's my brother.

He couldn't cope, depressed and sad
Please God, he begged, don't let me be bad
Darkness came, dimmed out the light
Somehow he lost the will to fight
     But he's my brother.

His body gone, his soul took flight
Gliding high, till out of sight
Please keep him safe, so he's not alone
Let him sit by you, as you hold the throne.
     Because he's my brother.

E Corr

THIS IS OUR FATE

Close your eyes
And hold my hand
Now think about
A promised land.

Our thoughts may take us
Past the stars
Beyond the place
We know as Mars.

Loosen the bind
It holds your mind
Unlock a dream
Then you will find.

The dream is a face
We long to see
He's waiting there
For you and me.

He knows our journey
Is shared with strife
And only reached
At the end of life.

At heaven's gate
Our Son will wait
For you and me
This is our fate.

Marie T Osborne

VICTORIA

This poem that I write is about a certain Queen
The longest serving monarch that there has ever been
Her reign it lasted for sixty four long years
At only eighteen years of age the crown was given hers
The impact she made was felt in every part of British life
She was such a loving mother a very devoted wife
Such dedication to her throne and country was clear to see
Her feelings she made clear within her voluminous diaries
She saw the British Empire extend to the far corners of the globe
Modern politics were born politicians had power they could hold
For Queen Victoria did not rule she reigned over this great land
She made her certain preferences very clear to understand
Her influence on her people was direct she was always on hand
Simplicity and her honesty in her manner set the tone
The nation responded and took her morals to their home
For she was like a mother to the people of her land
Her moral concept of her duty she did truly understand
The people turned to their queen the true symbol of the Victorian age
They celebrated unashamedly their patriotism they displayed
Two Jubilees she celebrated in this country she made great
But great sadness she did hold for she lost her beloved soulmate
For Victoria was devastated when her husband Albert died
She mourned for forty years until she was laid down at his side
Most people today have an image of a severe, old lady dressed in black
But we'll never have another Queen such as she except what history
Gives us back.

Elizabeth Leach

POET OF WORTH

The sad passing, in the year 1850 of William Wordsworth
A truly respected 'Man of Words;
Poet Laureate of high esteem
Devoted to 'his' beloved 'lakes'
Yes, I know
His passing was over a century ago
But a devout, family man.
Left behind a legacy
We should treasure and be thankful for
His poetry, you can imagine
The depth of his 'feelings'
When he put pen to paper
A treasured book
Letters, William Wordsworth wrote
To dear relatives and friends
A man of true understanding
A man of his time.

Margaret Parnell

LAMENT FOR BILL

'I want Bill,' said my aunt by marriage,
so we let her have him.
My aunt, wealthy and forbidding,
we, impoverished and humble,
dependent on my uncle for our home,
and Bill, my late grandmother's cat
the sacrificial victim:
snatched from the companionship of our own dog and cat
to languish in a London basement:
for he was too plebeian a creature
for my aunt's Pre-Raphaelite parlour.

A coward, I assented to this abduction,
and not until sixty-five years had passed
was I overcome by remorse.

Why didn't I speak out:-
'You shan't have him for a mere sentimental whim.'

Now I can only pray
that in some feline paradise
that resembles my grandmother's garden,
Bill is happily sporting with George and Marty.

E R Low

PUNCINELLO - AN ELEGY

Nothing I say can ever express
The agony of loss on that fateful day.
The day my beloved son was taken away . . .
Too young to go - so much to give -
He brought joy and comfort to all that he knew.
He was an anchor, support and best friend,
Part of my being will never mend.
We are but players upon life's stage,
A Puncinello . . .
       I must be brave.

Ivy Cawood

BEAUTY

I watch and wonder
I yearn and greed
I pray and hope
I need

I stare and focus
I look at U
You are so beautiful
If only U
Needed me too

You swallow
I breathe
You're a coward
I fall to my knees
You're unsure!
But, 'I am sure'
I want U

Tracy Charters

MY EPITAPH TO MY FRIEND SID

Let me paint you a picture in words,
Of an old Gentleman feeding his birds,
Picture an old armchair with Sid sitting there in his shed,
With his hands full of raisins saying, the birds must be fed,
He feeds them daily, they come to his plot,
And after he waits a while, he feeds the lot,
The Robin sits on the handle of his fork,
The Blackbirds and Sparrows came as if they were taught,
Sid was a gracious Gentleman, liked by everyone,
Also a loving Father to his Daughter and Son,
Everyone admired his garden,
His green fingers made all the flowers grow and grow
He was always there to help you that's why he was loved so,
His home was neat and shining,
His brass complimented Mabel's lovely white nets,
He was a Bowler and a Sportsman to every player he met,
We could go on forever about his kindness and care,
But sadly life only lasts a lifetime and the time was very near,
He loved his wife Mabel and always gave her tea in bed,
One morning he gave her an extra cuddle making her think why?
Little did she realise she would know by and by,
And hours later she found he'd fallen in his shed,
He left behind great sorrow but also lots of cheer,
For his memory is one of the greatest,
Trying to live up to this is one's utmost test.

Jan Graver-Wild

REMEMBER ROY
(For Dawn)

Hi one day, bye the next
How can it happen
Why did he die?
No warning, Good Morning
A normal start to the day.

They said it was a heart attack
Don't be silly he'll be back
He's her dad she loves him
He wouldn't leave her, it's just a whim.

Well it happened, he died, Roy was his name
Yes, it was true, it wasn't a game
Now she's alone and wondering why
She really did love her dad, that's no lie.

Sharon Stewart

DAVID

The man who died was fifty-three, he'd led a simple life.
He'd worked and bred and loved and daily shaved his face.
He wasn't bright, he wasn't dull, just middle of the road,
A family man, a friend, an elder in the church.

You couldn't talk with him about ideas, of Proust, Monet or Bach.
He had no maths, no cultured conversation
and yet he filled his space.
I loved him dear, his simple face, his skin of healthy hue.
And I could be with him for hours in silent harmony.

And now he's gone, his eyes are closed, all happened in a month.
What is the plan, the logic here? Why is his life curtained?
I felt a presence in his soul, a halo of content
and though I wasn't close to him, I'll miss him with my guts.

Some mystic sense of special grace, I sensed it in his being.
His daughter put it succinctly in words of simple truth,
he's called to God my mother dear to do a special job.

Jack Oliver

A TRIBUTE TO OLIVE

Goodnight dear Mother and our beloved Nan.
Your eyes closed for the last time, God had held out his hands.

Into his grasp you bravely walked. Left us all speechless unable to talk.

As the tears streamed down from our eyes.
Was it such a bad thing that you had died?
To watch you suffer was too much to bear
God made a decision that at first seemed unfair.

But as we reflected on your life in the past
You weren't the same person who could make us all laugh!

None of us strong enough to see you in pain.
To wish you to stay longer was purely our gain.

Now you're in Heaven smiling down from above
Filling our hearts with buckets of love.

We have our memories of the good times we shared
And have the comfort of knowing that one day we will again be paired.

Our loss will be comforted in many ways,
Especially as you were taken from us on the Holiest of days.

Tracy Brightman

NANNA

I feel you are still near
Certain sounds and smells
Make my head turn
And I expect you to be there.
But you're not
And a part of me knows that
You will never be there again.
It's just in my mind
I can't quite believe that
I'll never see you.

Maybe you are near
Maybe keeping an eye on
Your great-granddaughter
And how she's growing
As she always made you smile
And a small kiss from her
Would light your face
And take years from you.
Your body thrived on her being near
As if her youth could revive you
But at the end of the day
When we were gone
Age crept up and clasped your shoulder once more
If only she could have been near you at the end
Maybe her youth could have kept you here
Even just for a few more years
Just long enough to see her grow into
The child she has now become
But maybe you have seen her
Maybe she sees you
And I'm too blind to notice.

Claire Sanderson

TO A BROTHER I NEVER KNEW
(Victor James Wilkins 1927 - 1929)

To me you were just an urn
Atop a grass-covered grave
That Mother hacked at with the garden shears
She never said much
'He was our first baby
He would have been a big boy now!'
Some old creased black and white photos
Hand-me-down baby clothes
That Grandma still had kept
And an urn atop a grave
That Mother hacked at with the garden shears
Some Saturday mornings
After doing the shopping down town
I didn't speak
Mother said nothing
Just kept on hacking
With those rusty, old shears
On Saturday mornings
After doing the shopping
Down town.

Paul Wilkins

THE HARRY ELEGY

The Harry, he was a houseboat barge
Painted white with gold face and stern
Proud and stately, many an eye-opener
For sightseers on the Brayford Basin Wharf
In the Fosse Dyke river in Lincoln
His hold was a lounge with
A baby grand piano, settees
Placed to see the sky through
The pane glass windows with
An ample galley and four bunk
Bedrooms, so very cosy to reside in.

The Harry's master died
He was left alone
Though sometimes a close friend
Of his master's came to pump the bilges
But even that help when it stopped
Left The Harry in a dire state
And finally, he sank until only his face and stern
Upperstructure remained visible.

The Harry became an eyesore
No longer was he admired
By bypassers by along the Bradford Basin Wharf
He was thought of as, a hazard to the Bradford Basic traffic
So he was, dragged up,
Emptied of his stagnant water
And towed by tug to an
Isolated part of the Fosse Dyke
And when his watercock was opened
The Harry came to rest on the bottom of the dyke
Forlorn and forever forgotten!

Alma Montgomery Frank

POEM

People say I'll see you when I'm at peace myself,
But I don't know for sure if heaven is true,
But if Heaven is true, I know for sure that is where you have gone
Because whenever your name is mentioned
Everyone's face lights up with a smile
And I know that they are thinking happy thoughts
And loving thoughts which makes me think of my
Loving Dad
Who is gone forever
But will never be forgotten.

Patsy McMenamin

AN ELEGY TO A LOVELY FRIEND

Oh how I hate this world sometimes
It all seems so unfair
Someone we love and care about
Confined to a wheelchair.

She loved the Vales of Scotland most
Met her family, yearly there
And now her time is running out
It does seem so unfair.

She doesn't feel remorse herself
So happy with her life
Battling on from dawn to dusk
Content, despite her strife.

Oh how our feelings contrast with life
Hopes and aspirations dashed
We wanted a miracle, but in vain
It seems our world has crashed.

Oh how I hate this world sometimes
You can't give God a dare
His will, not ours we must accept
Makes life seem so unfair.

Our hearts will break we know it
Our feelings so sincere
But others are hurting more than us
For them we shed our tears.

We hoped our love would see her through
Our energies we'd share
Let laughter hide our heavy hearts
A sham, so hard to bear.

But we will love the world again
Spurred on by thoughts and dreams
Sweet memories of our lovely friend
Because love wins in the end.

Brian Hurll

ELEGY FOR STRINGS

Sad, is the song of the violin
Echoing the *cello's* throbbing pain,
Reflecting in their torment
The anguish in my heart,
For you are gone . . .
And I'm alone, again.

Bittersweet, is the music
Of the plaintive violin,
Haunting . . . as the *cello's* deep lament,
Plucking at my heartstrings
And in my desolation
Recalling days I thought could never end.

Summertime is over -
Winter's chill benumbs my soul,
What use the tears I scorn,
But can't restrain?

Yet . . . Spring must follow Winter
Sure as dark clouds flee the sun,
And Time will heal . . .
And I'll know joy . . . again.

Elizabeth Amy Johns

PROOF OF LOVE

My boyfriend Mark
Cycles in the wind and rain, daylight and dark.

Visiting me
Is a journey of six miles
So Mark takes a shortcut over field and stiles.

He's not cycling for health
But for love of me
As I'm disabled to a certain degree.

I've courted Mark for half a year
Although being disabled, I'm loved for myself
He's made that quite clear.

When Mark arrives
His clothes, sometimes are wet through
I've known him still cycle, inflicted with the flu.

Mark uses his cycle every day
As West Midlands travel he doesn't have to pay.

With money saved
He purchases posies
Last time it was a bunch of red roses.

When together we are like love birds
As the saying goes
Actions speak a lot louder than words.

Come hail, wind, rain or shine
I'm more than glad, that man is mine.

Yvonne Bacon

LOVE REMEMBERED

You don't stop loving someone,
Just because they're dead.
Leaving affection in your heart,
And memories in your head.
    It's only natural to have thoughts,
    Of a love that's unsurpassed.
    When you count the times you vowed,
    Your love will always last.
Time may only temper feelings,
At losing a life you shared.
But, perhaps, there was a reason,
Why you alone were spared.
    Maybe, it's because your heart,
    Has other loves in store.
    Tho' each is a different kind
    To the love you gave before.

Harry Walker

LOVE HOLDS ON

I can't let go of you
I feel you in my heart,
Love holds on
And never breaks apart.

I have got love for you,
More than you'll ever know,
Love holds on,
So you, I won't let go.

I show love in my writing
An all I do and say,
Love holds on,
So you'll never get away.

This love I feel,
It feels so right,
Love holds on,
Through the day and night.

I think of you,
In all of my dreams,
Love holds on,
Well so it seems.

When I'm with you,
I'm happy as can be,
Love holds on, I hope,
You'll never set me free.

Mondo

WHY THE WHY'S?

Why did your love
Have to fade
Why didn't it last
As it was made?
Why do the birds
In my heart, no longer sing?
Why all this heartache
Did you bring?
Why this gut feeling
Of attack, attack?
Why do I feel
I must hold back?
Why don't you hear
Our daughter's cries?
Why are all these questions
Starting with why's?
Because in my heart
I love you true
Perhaps one day
You'll love me, as I love you.
You must know
I'll always yearn
And I'll pray
For your return
To live in hope
Will always be
That one day
You'll come home, to me.

Jason Davies

ONE DAY...

Fixated by the glance
That happened, out of chance,
They glared before they danced,
This was to be,
Their first true romance.

Always knowing
Still so prolonged
Cheeks close and glowing
As they danced to their song.

Dreamland alive
Their wishes come true,
Together they will thrive
If only, he knew . . .

Donna Hardie

VALENTINE'S DAY DEVOTION

Love, kindness and companionship I sought in life,
Many girls later one finally became my wife.
There is one thing to remember though, you have faults too,
And with this kept in mind, your relationship will win through.

John P Evans

I WISH . . .

When did you ever read my mind?
Do I remember when you were kind?
Now I sat beside you and I was your find
But sometimes I wish that I had always been blind.

P Allen

SLUMBER RESUMED

The ending awaited
By you and by him
Unfurls without hesitation
An explosion of comprehension
Shadows and doubt
Silver linings erased
Dreams cast at a time
With no fear of rejection
The truth is confusing
Half expected at heart
The show of affection
The foreboding mistake
To have kept back full feelings
To enhance the full chase
Captured is dull
The challenge is melted
To rekindle the flames
An attempt made half-hearted
Sitting back waiting
With many beers down
Acceptance invades the deepest recesses
At ease and at peace
A tingle of hope sends a shiver
Resilience of heartache
Which makes us much stronger
Experiences tell us
And help us to grow
So until the next time
His head will say *No!*

Andrew Tatam

PORTRAIT OF YOU

I'll paint a picture of love for you dear
Without I hope shedding a tear
Starting with the background the sky of blue
I feel this when I am not with you.
Dip the brush into shades of green
Jealousy creeps through but can't be seen
Hair of brown blowing in the breeze
Disappearing among the trees
Oval face painted pinky white
Eyes of blue twinkle in the light
A mouth filled in with blushing red
Suggesting love 'Let's go to bed.'
Shading the nose not to make it big or small
Two ears now so I can hear you call
A tiny grin to make me smile
It always lasts a long, long while
Your neck and shoulders to hold your head high
Sending a message of love to fill up the sky
Two arms to wrap around me so tight
Keeping me warm in the middle of the night
Now too your chest with a heart hidden away
Softly beating through night and day
Next your stomach I colour with grace
This pleases you by the look on your face
Two long legs with muscles, just some
They are holding up your bum
Your feet I paint filled in with pride
Senses all the moves you take in your stride
The picture is finished I will clear up the mess
And put my feet up and take a rest
I shall frame this picture so we can recall
Every time we glance upon the wall.

Jan Nice

IN THE PURSUIT OF LOVE

I have seen what you hide with a mask of stone
I have gazed upon your weeping heart
And though I must remove your throne
It is so we will never be apart.

Your challenge I accept with honour and glee
My pursuit will flower your love
And we both know who the winner will be
By the greatest fight for my dove.

We knew it was too good to last
We ended up saying 'goodbye'
And when I begin to face the past
A tear it brings to my eye.

Alex Mcleod

MURIEL'S MEMORIES

I often think about you and the life we used to share
Your photos all around me to me you're always there
I think about your loving ways the way you always shared
Being always just for me when I thought nobody cared
Fighting all my battles making a cup of tea
Making sure I was always first enjoying the security
Of feeling safe always just knowing you were near
My soulmate and companion to me you were so dear
Always holding tight my hand when we went for a walk
Being my own confidante when we used to talk
Always kind and caring I was always number one
How I miss those bygone days now that you are gone
But I have wonderful memories that no one can take away
My darling Doug you still live on - *in my heart every day.*

Jean Beardsmore

IN FONDEST MEMORY . . .

Will you wonder, when the years have flown,
What became of me, your one-time love?
For whom the seeds of romance, lightly sown,
Have long since dispersed, to higher realms above.

Might you ponder, through the lonely night,
When all your thoughts dwell upon me,
Why our fledgling romance took its flight
And never bore fruit, as was meant to be.

Are you fonder, even now, of another,
Yet still your dreams are all my own,
And did she become your children's mother
Who, like my own, the nest have flown?

Ah, what might have been, had destiny
Decreed that we two were never set free.

Julia Eva Yeardye

LOVE AFFAIR

Now looking decidedly old
Yet still fitting comfortably, I'm told
Her constant companion and always there
Giving warmth and comfort everywhere.
No amount of pleading to change to new
Would make her alter her view
For it was part of her past
When things were made to last.
So she preferred to cherish and wear
Her creation of a yesteryear
Although showing signs of age
At this late stage
She wore it with pride
And took criticism in her stride
Cosily it had protected her from ill
And many a sudden chill
Making a bond between them tight
Even though not a pretty sight
But as a mere man dare I say
That women are delightfully different that way
For it was as a young girl the affair began
When my wife knitted her favourite cardigan.

Alan M Duncan

LOST LOVE!

Standing on the whispering sands
Beside a sea of tears
Waiting for the tide to turn
To vanquish all my fears.

Time is such a precious gift
We have so little of
Life's one big adventure
Of stories filled with love.

But silence shatters many dreams
As bitter rain fades out the light
Passions lost in memories
Never knowing wrong from right.

We caress the stars with twinkling eyes
From truth we hide our shame
Love is like a deck of cards
Many players lose their game.

They stand alone on the whispering sand
Their tears fall on the beach
All as one with such memories
For a love that's beyond all reach . . .

GIG

MEMORIES

Today I walk with you my love
O'er the sand dunes near the sea
With memories of youth and fun
And our hearts were free
Today I walk alone, those times are no more
Loneliness will end, as I join you
            on God's golden shore
Hand in hand together, as in life we were
Tho' you are so far away, my heart is with you there.

Amy Savage

BLUE FIRE
(To ACEM)

See each facet, how it gleams,
Burns within its depths blue fire,
A diamond is forever,
An object of desire.

True love with many a facet gleams,
And deep within there burns a flame,
A diamond is forever,
May our love remain the same.

Pauline Wilkins

MISTY

High above the clouds
You smile
With sunshine in your eyes
I know you never cry
For rainbows in the sky
Though the blue is misty
I will see you.

Helen Owen

GIVE A SMILE

A smile is such a simple thing,
But so much happiness, it can bring,
To a special loved one, to whom you greet,
Or to an unknown person, seen in the street,
If you put to good use, this wonderful gift,
You may be surprised how soon your spirits lift,
So pass on a smile, to someone today,
And happiness will soon brighten your day.

Clare Allen

DADDY I NEED YOU . . .

Daddy I need you . . .

to be all that You say You are.
to be so delighted with me that You will always love me.
to be so jealous of me that You will always protect me.
to be so proud of me that You will never deny me.
to be so happy to spend time with me.
to be so eager to teach and guide me.
to be so merciful over honest mistakes.
to be so tender and sing Your songs of love over me.
to be so confident that You can complete the work of Jesus in me.
to be so willing to lift me up if I stumble.
to be so faithful to constantly watch over me.
to be so available when I have no one else to turn to.
to be so gentle when my heart is breaking within me.
to be so consistent when life is falling apart around me.
to be so funny when true humour would lift my spirit.
to be so unendingly patient with me.
to be so big when fear grips little me.
to be so open-handed with Your grace for empty me.
to be so powerful to enable me.
to be my shelter when the storm surrounds me.
to be all and more than I ever imagined You to be . . .

in my humanity!

Margi Hughes

FRIENDS

Laughter is a gift.
When they laugh I feel amazing
Dancing feel the rhythm.
From the top of your head to the bottom of your toes.
Music makes our world go round.
Amusement rides never get restless of the thrill.
Youth a precious thing!
That should be used wildly, not wisely.
Money, spend it carelessly.
Until your teen spirit drips dry.
Laugh at the most inappropriate times.
Some days get away from it all.
We run carelessly through fields.
Cows' dung everywhere.
Don't cringe, laugh loudly.
Like we do!
Lay by a river
As we wake nature, and think of our future.
And laugh at the top of our voices about the past.
When we were younger, we were the same as today.
You don't have to change!
Bad, terrible things happen, but we get through it with a smile.
As we grow, we shall progress, so progress.
We will venture out, but something will pull us back.
To that river, our river so make a river!
And there you will think of your future.
And laugh at the top of your voices about the past.

Charlotte Western-Reed

NEVER FEAR NEVER FEAR

There is always something to sing for
While hearts make the beat after beat
Songs are born of rapture or fear
Never fear never fear
The songs live on
When the fear has gone.

There is always something to hope for
While breath keeps the uh-huh rhythm.
Songs are born of gladness or fear
Never fear never fear
The songs live on
When the fear has gone.

There is always something to work for
While songs belong to everyone.
Songs may tell of a working life
Of the daily run
The songs live on
When the work is done.

To sing and hope and work and fret,
So well known the theme of life.
Songs are born of rapture or fear
Never fear never fear
The songs live on
When the fear has gone.

Doris Payne

TRUE LOVE, DAUGHTER IN LAW

We dreamt of having a daughter
Though one we never had
Until our son brought you home
This really made us glad
We kissed you and we loved you
Showed you that we care
Thanked our lucky stars
For this life, we came to share.

'Twas when you lit that love flame
So deep down in our heart
How could we ever imagine
The time would come to part
We miss you and we love you
For all that it's worth
To us you're very special
Our treasure, of this earth.

Hoping yes we're hoping
You will not severe the ties
Perhaps one day you will listen
To our saddened heartache cries
Because dreams are easily shattered
And end with a tear or two
Now we never dream for a daughter
In our dreams, we dream of you.

Dennis N Davies

EMILY SCARLETT'S SMILE

It brightens up my day
It fills me up with love
My daughter's smile is perfect
She's my angel from above.

A small face, a smile so big,
My heart it fills with pure delight,
When I look at her and she smiles at me
My absolute favourite sight.

Lynsey Werney

IN EVERY THOUGHT

In every thought a story,
In every bell a chime,
In every chime a song.
And sunshine steals the morning glory.
And dewdrops twinkle in the glow
And melodies meet the morning,
And all the birds are in full throat.
As morning breaks the music floats.
The pageant and the merry notes,
The night time curtain drawn aside,
Now begins the day.
And cast, all dressed, perform the play,
The play of life, the play of day.
Full spotlight on the stage,
The sun casts down its rays,
And enter now the acting players,
And each one tells his single tale.
Each painted face, each mask,
Each different garb, each new disguise,
Each performance on the stage,
Lit by the rays of the sun,
And prompted by the wind's soft whisper,
And each new player on the stage,
Tells his tale of life.

J Blissett

THE WAY

Jesus taught them
in that day.
People who were
of the 'way.'

Many lived long
years ago . . .
Believing what he said
was so . . .

Jesus said 'I am the way,
the way, the truth, and life.
It could be the same today . . .
If folks would lay aside
their strife . . .

Jesus Christ, the peaceful one,
God's very own beloved Son . . .
He always said 'Fret not' . . .
He brings peace, and cares a lot . . .

If we would hearken unto His voice . . .
Even today we can make a choice . . .
Whether we want to belong to 'The way
we could decide on this very day . . .

Carol Olson

MEDITATION

If your life is full of stress,
You feel you live under duress,
And seek that inner happiness,
Then learn to Meditate.

If you lack the urge to get things done,
Hopes for the future you have none -
See only clouds and not the sun,
Then learn to Meditate.

If you fear you may forget
The things you have to do or get,
No need to worry or to fret,
Just learn to Meditate.

If you seek yet cannot find,
If you wish for peace of mind,
And peace on earth for all mankind,
Then let us Meditate.

Valerie Small

COUNT YOUR BLESSINGS

'Count your blessings,' so the song says,
This we can do in so many ways,
When we are fortunate to have good health,
It's worth far more than untold wealth.

To be free to come and go as we choose,
Our own lives to live, with nothing to lose.
How many people in the world today.
Would like such a choice, if they had their say.

The meeting of friends, as we go on our way.
The greetings we exchange which brighten our day.
The glorious colours of sunset what a splendid sight,
Before darkness falls, ere comes the night.

To have loving family by your side,
In times of trouble, to help and to guide.
The beauties of nature, all seen at a glance,
With blossom and flowers our lives to enhance.

The winter landscape, when covered in snow,
Making our hearts and fingers glow,
Cascading waterfalls down mountainside,
Watching from cliff-top, the ever changing tide.

How fortunate we are, these gifts that are free,
God's blessings in life, for you and for me.

E Kathleen Jones

LIFE IS A JOURNEY

Life is a journey
So travel it well
Make the most
Of the years yet to come
It will be the greatest
Adventure of all
From the days
We were terribly young
It's a journey of laughter
Of happiest days
It is joy and
Great pleasures untold
Yes life is a journey
So travel it well
It's a story as each day enfolds.

Jeanette Gaffney

PEAS ABOVE STICKS

I am green with envy
So I need to improve,
I'm gonna bang my drum,
Get into a winning groove.

Gonna work on my performance
And hone up all my skills, I'll do a balcony scene,
On star-laden window sills.

Could be a pea on a drum
Or a flaming firestick,
A flea on an elephant's back
Or a worker of magic.

How things will turn out,
I really don't know.
I'll jump in feet first,
And just go with the flow.

Am I better or worse,
Than I think I am?
I really must find out,
And begin to understand.

I am green with envy,
That will serve to inspire.
I will create not imitate,
My high flown dreams flying higher.

Ian Barton

EVER COMPANION

You accompany me everywhere
Countryside, seaside,
In all my waking thoughts
My poems you in mind abide.

Wherever I happen to be you're there
Ever-companion,
Awaiting your inspiration,
Through you I feel champion.

You transport me into the right dreams,
Staying by my side,
Confident, assuring,
Pressures will not get wide.

Sending me on a romantic ecstasy,
You bring me back down,
Conquering the world for me,
Poem, my companion noun.

Made for each other we, you describe
The colour of love,
To me love is you my poems
It's so clear you're sent from above.

Magically enveloping my heart
Love feelings and kiss
Filling my pen with sweet words
No trace of evil or prejudice.

Making sure I keep busy as
Our little Bo-peep,
Never satisfied,
You want to invade my sleep.

But so lost I'd be without your
Good companionship,
Of Browning, Tennyson block,
You're determined I'll be a chip.

Barbara Sherlow

ONE OF THOSE DAYS

Is it one of those days,
when nothing goes right?
You've got a sore head,
Been awake half the night.
There's washing to do,
the dinner to make,
And the cat's on the table,
it's licking the cake.

'Get off there you nuisance!'
Now it's wanting fed.
It miaows in a huff
and stalks off to its bed.
'Wish I could do that!'
But there's dusting to do,
I wonder if I should prepare,
a soup or stew?'

The dog's in the flower bed.
It's digging again.
Much as I love him,
sometimes he's a pain.
You dust and you vacuum
you season the stew,
the washing is fluttering
out in the blue.

The kids will be home,
with a hug and a kiss.
'Ah' life isn't so bad.
There's worse fates than this.

Isobel Laffin

EARLY TO BED, EARLY TO RISE

I'm glad I wake up early
That way I get things done
And sometimes on a good day
Life can be rather fun.
Then when I get a bad day,
Old weary and sad.
I wait for better weather
And don't feel quite so bad.

Emily Apps

OUT OF THE DOLDRUMS?

Feeling in the doldrums? Reach for some
Paper and a pen,
Let your feelings and emotions run free
Every now and then,
You could write a story, or a short poem instead.
You'll be surprised how quickly words
Come into your head,
You can sail the seven seas, pretend
That you are anywhere,
Let your mind wander from your cosy armchair,
And when you've finished writing and
Joined the human race,
I'm sure you'll be sitting there with
A smile upon your face.

Hazell Dennison

BIRTHDAY

This birthday I'm fifty-four
A long time since I had the key of the door.
Thirty three years in fact on the fifth of May
It's all down hill now some might say.
More wrinkles now I trace
With a finger down my face.
At the hairdressers I have to pay
More money to cover my grey.
My body that was once slim
Kept its shape neat and trim
Has started on this middle age spread
Those words I have come to dread.
A gentle brush is all I give
As my teeth are sensitive
At least I have a full set
So things are not that bad yet.
I don't want to grow old and graceful
I want to be hip and cool, not dull.
Although some of me has gone to pot
I'm quite happy with my lot.
Some days I'm full of beans
Then my husband knows what that means,
Now and then he's in for a treat
Me? I prefer a sweet,
Sweets last longer than two ticks
Still you can't teach an old dog new tricks.
I'm going to have a great birthday
Enjoy myself come what may
I can still manage to jive
Good heavens! Next year I'll be fifty-five.

Patricia Whorwood

WHEN LIFE GIVES YOU LEMONS

When your heart pumps only sand
and you can feel the tear-tide waxing,
don't Canute-ish raise a hand
but focus on relaxing.

Let those burning breakers rush
across disappointment's pain-baked shore;
build sand-castles in the hush,
gifted when you cry no more.

Stare into a deep rock-pool
and make faces at your reflection.
If you laugh . . . it's not a fool
skirts rip-tides of dejection.

If these tactics should all fail
amidst the gales of SAD or sorrow,
there's one truth to keep you hale:
who knows what comes tomorrow?

Perry McDaid

IN HER WORLD

Sitting, in her flat, alone . . .
And on the phone to me,
She felt she had to explain
'When you rang me, earlier . . .
I'm sorry if I sounded a bit down. But,
I never tell anybody, today
Is the birthday of the baby daughter I lost.
She would have been forty-three'

'Catherine,' I said. 'A miscarriage.
She died . . . two days later. I remember.'

She said, 'I had to get out this morning,
I needed some cigarettes . . .
When that . . . feeling comes . . .
I had to get out.
Is it just . . . with me . . .
I never tell anybody.'
'Not even your two sons?' I asked.
'I never tell. Never.'

'We'll celebrate Catherine's birthday,' I said.
'I'll light a candle. You do the same.
We'll keep a candle burning,
For her, all day long.
She would have been forty-three.
No grave. Just you still thinking of her . . .
You and me - today.
I'll light a candle. You do the same.
Catherine had uniqueness in her mind.'

Claire-Lyse Sylvester

MIDDLE-AGE SPREAD

Insidious: creeping; Those extra rolls and creases that appear when
I'm sleeping. Magazines call it middle-age spread; But oh how I dread
being in middle age; Oh how I rage at writing out lists the sly reminders
that my memory plays tricks.

Celebrities know how to turn back the clock to stay young and in tune,
supple and slender. They have face lifts and tummy tucks; They don't
go on a bender of Newcastle Brown down the Old Dog and Duck; Or
eat chocolate fudge cake with thick double cream. A cholesterol
nightmare: A menopausal dream.

Middle-age is really a terrible bore. Night after night stuck in front of
the telly with the grumbling groans of a diet fed belly.
So I've made my decision I'll accept my lot. Grey hair and wrinkles?
I'll not care a jot. I'll eat till I'm full; ignore my sagging turn and bum;
And blame it all on the gravitational pull.

Chris Senior

IF ONLY I COULD SLEEP

Baffling little puzzles of great mind bending qualities swim
inside my head.
Whilst supposedly my mind should be calm and resting in the
hours that I occupy my bed.
Activity seems all around my body and in my mind
relaxation is called for if I'm ever to unwind.

I'm just a nervous person constantly on pins,
looking to the future, I'll try again, perhaps mind over matter, wins.
Baffling little puzzles of great mindbending qualities swim inside my
head.
Perhaps it's all the books and information I have gathered up and read.
Sleep will come, no doubt, but at a later hour.
At the present moment I have not got the power,
to sleep like an infant wrapped in a cocoon.
In the warmth and quietness of its mother's womb.

May be I'm a dreamer of dreams that come and go.
Perhaps I have slept a while, I simply do not know.
Anyhow I am now awake once more and feeling fine,
so sorry to have rowed last night with that dear husband of mine.
So in future I'll make it up with him before I go to bed,
Then no more baffling little puzzles of great mind bending qualities
will swim inside my head.

Pamela M Wild